Fix the Van!

By Carmel Reilly

T0360132

Vic the pet vet has a van.

Her van can not go!

I can fix it, Vic!

Val and her dog Kip
zip to see Vic.

Val has a box of van bits.

Kip pops six van bits in a zip bag.

Kip tips the zip bag
into the bin.

CHECKING FOR MEANING

1. Why did Vic call Val? *(Literal)*

2. What did Val use to fix the van? *(Literal)*

3. Why didn't Val want to mix up the bits? *(Inferential)*

EXTENDING VOCABULARY

mix	What are different meanings of this word? Can you use *mix* in a sentence to show a different meaning?
yip and **yap**	What do these words mean in the text? Which sounds in the words are the same? Which are different?
six	What is the meaning of this word? If you take away the letter *s*, what other letter can you put at the start to make a new word?

MOVING BEYOND THE TEXT

1. What name do we give to a person who fixes cars, trucks and big machines?

2. What are some tools this person might use?

3. How do people learn to fix cars and vans?

4. What would you be able to teach another person if they asked you for help?

SPEED SOUNDS

Xx	Yy	Zz

Kk	Ll	Vv	Qq	Ww
Dd	Jj	Oo	Gg	Uu

Cc	Bb	Rr	Ee	Ff	Hh	Nn
Mm	Ss	Aa	Pp	Ii	Tt	

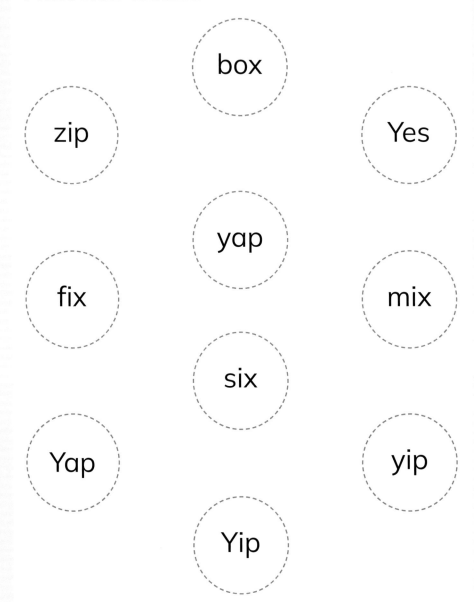

box

zip

Yes

yap

fix

mix

six

Yap

yip

Yip